It's Hard Enough to Fly

It's Hard Enough to Fly

Poems by

Donald Wheelock

© 2022 Donald Wheelock. All rights reserved.
This material may not be reproduced in any form, published,
reprinted, recorded, performed, broadcast,
rewritten or redistributed without
the explicit permission of Donald Wheelock.
All such actions are strictly prohibited by law.

Cover design by Shay Culligan
Cover art by Jay DeMartine, *Big Spenser Mountain*
Author photo by Anne Wheelock

ISBN: 978-1-63980-157-2

Kelsay Books
502 South 1040 East, A-119
American Fork, Utah 84003
Kelsaybooks.com

Acknowledgments

Coming late to the publishing of poetry, I have benefitted from the critical and editorial advice of many people over the past few years. Foremost among these is Deborah Warren. For her insights and suggestions I am especially grateful. She has been for some time a favorite of mine among the living practitioners of formal poetry, and I hope some of what she has so beautifully mastered in her own art has rubbed off on me.

I am grateful to the editors of these publications in which these poems, or earlier versions of them, first appeared or are forthcoming.

Blue Unicorn: "A Fortune Turned," "Credo in Short Sentences," "Hunger and the Hawk"
Ekphrasis: "On the Yacht Namouna"
Equinox: "Wake"
Grand Little Things: "Pilot Light"
Jelly Bucket: "Blackbird on a Cattail," "Baltimore Visitors, 2021"
Linea: "Billowing Sails," "To Find the World," "Stone Cottage"
New English Review: "Nap," "Snow Patches in Rain," "Just the Bay," "Notes from Underground," "Unearthing My Fossil," "More Word than Meaning"
Quadrant Magazine: "Background Music," "Scandal"
Rue Scribe: "Not Far from Here," "Broken Glass"
Snakeskin: "Compose a Fugue: A Practical Guide," "Their World"
Sparks of Calliope: "Hopper's *Dories*"
The Author's Journal of Inventive Literature: "Outcasts"
The Lyric: "Fog"
The Road Not Taken: "Eighty's the New Sixty," "Meeting on the Stairs"
Think: "Proper Nouns Are the First to Go," "Winter Room," "Obituary Picture, 2021"

Third Wednesday: "Boot Jack"
Verse-Virtual: "March Ahead," "A Sailing Out from Life,"
    "Settling"

Four of the poems printed here appeared in my chapbook, *In the Sea of Dreams,* Gallery of Readers Press: "Wake," "Outcasts," "Highboy," and "Alone." Three of these have also appeared in journals, as noted above.

Contents

Billowing Sails   13

I. Sea Fog

To Find the World   17
Hopper's *Dories*   18
Outcasts   19
Fog   20
Plus One Makes Four   21
Summer Rental   25
On the Yacht Namouna   26
Heart   28
Stone Cottage   29
Winter Room   30
Nap   31
Snow Patches in Rain   32

II. Mind's Eye

Mind's Eye   35
Pilot Light   36
Highboy   37
Going, Going, Gone   38
Antiques   39
Boot Jack   40
From Where This Silence Settled   41
More Word than Meaning   42
Train Travel   43
Dreamless Sleep   44

III. Unearthing My Fossil

Life: Darwin Explained	47
The Grand Cannibal	48
Hunger and the Hawk	49
Credo in Short Sentences	50
Notes from Underground	51
Unearthing My Fossil	52
A Sailing Out from Life	56

IV. Flight

Hummingbird	59
Blackbird on a Cattail	60
Fish	61
Their World	62
Testing North in February	63
Above the Arctic Ice	64
Baltimore Visitors, 2021	65

V. Settling on the View

Meeting on the Stairs	69
Divestiture	70
Proper Nouns Are the First to Go	71
Eighty's the New Sixty	72
Spring Day, 2020	73
March Ahead	74
Obituary Picture, 2021	75
Is Every Death Our Own?	76
Alone	77
Settling	78

Sculpture Garden	79
Refrain	80
Wake	81

VI. Column Two

A Fortune Turned	85
Not Far from Here	86
Broken Glass	87
Scandal	88
Background Music	89
Compose a Fugue: A Practical Guide	90
Noon to Midnight	91
Just the Bay	92

Billowing Sails

To launch with billowing sails
a course aimed true, in sight,
well-rhymed, concise, entails
   lines hauled in tight.

I. Sea Fog

To Find the World

There must be something more to write about
than goings-on outside my favorite window
—something significant, if not that certain;
what if a war were in the news, a drought?
The stunning tones of spring won't let them in, though.
To find the world I'd have to draw the curtain.

Hopper's *Dories*

after Edward Hopper, The Dories, Ogunquit,
Whitney Museum of American Art

Attentive to the forces of the tide,
they point up into open ocean breeze
like hungry pets anticipating food.
They feel the breeze enliven what they see.
A distant shore encloses open sea.

A view of coast as crisp and deep as life
itself, before the smudges of mankind
applied a slick to every shore and reef;
even the clouds are swept clean by the wind.

Feathery skies of sun-made summer choose
a clear-eyed, optimistic morning view
to paint the cove profusions of its blues.

The froth of distant ocean surf and light
explodes into the dory-sides as white.

Outcasts

Out past a sandy spit on Scott
an isolated heap of rock
asserts itself above low tide.
A dozen spruce at least as tall
as such a crowded place is small
cling to this fundament of stone,
huddling in a scrim together,
unmoved, unsheltered from the weather.

To eyes only one Maine cove away
they'd seem at any time of day
outcasts, all, from coastal spruce,
as if this ledge had broken loose
by some unfriendly will of trees.

Years established, they reproduce
through summer drought and winter gale,
hoping a rooted stubbornness
will yield a modest plot of soil.

Thus exiled, they hold their own,
these rigid conifers no stone
can cast aside, resigned to face
the life this uncharitable place
reserves for salt, sea air and wind,
to cling to, there, the stone-dark ground.

Fog

A second sea rolls in, this air
beneath the sky, a tide above
the silent movements of the cove,
as if a lonely thoroughfare

of thought had taken on the task
of wearing on its land, the sea,
the doleful and suspended tree
a temporary formless mask.

It keeps my thoughts on ground,
but where no evidence of place
should bar imaginary space
from claiming mind. Now, only sound

can penetrate this dense, grey light:
the horn, the isolated bell,
the solitary, careworn gull
disconsolate in unseen flight.

A curtain for the soul, this calm
obscures with veiled eternity
the world's horizons, blinding me
to show me who and where I am.

Plus One Makes Four

The island from the air:
oyster-shaped, its shores
scalloped where the bluffs
support hotels, their stairs
descending to the rough
and rock-assaulting surf.

We shared our father with
one fifty-second of the year—
one week with him was ours,
but one we also had to share
with his small orchestra,
rich and shrill—and *her*.

Our music to collective ears—
every phrase and trill
played straight from every heart—
resembled Haydn, poor Mozart,
and Dvorak, less than we,
in a fairer world, would like.

The word we never voiced:
girlfriend, unsuitable we felt
for friends of men his age;
he flew her in to share; the act
abused the day, the week. Our needs
left little room for hourly screeds,

compulsive talk, oblivious
to any but her need to fill
the space between us, like tar
late-winter potholes. Still,
in retrospect, she must have had
as many nervous urges

to commandeer the talk,
as adolescent boys
to wish her swift removal.
Even with a room full
of cocktail people, the noise
proved insufficient to the task.

Sea, sand, music, sun,
ingredients for a recipe of fun
for boys hungry for a week away;
add: time to get to know a man
we barely knew, the one,
were ours another family—say,

the Joneses or the Smiths—
we'd share our meals with still.
Now ice cream fills the bill:
Have what you want, boys,
among the parlor's list of pleasures,
a father the cherry on the top.

Plus one makes four, to tell
how memories of ice cream
applied to every member
of her family, her friends,
Bill and Little Bill—we males
as still as bookends in academe.

That everyone accepts her
doesn't help: from a favorite player,
an advocate: *She's a peach*.
Next year she won't be missed
if the boys have anything to say.
Music's Greek to her, Greek

who knows what. A tart
retort draws the icy stare,
his reprimand, revives
the chills from childhood.
If only she weren't there.
But wishes fail as wishes should,

at least when wishing others
future ill: we'll face a man struck
to stone…
        Had I that week again,
I'd welcome her that day,
but who could know tragedy absolute
would take him soon away

with a single stroke? Devotion
is tending half a marriage
to an invalid struck almost dumb,
a wheelchair for a carriage,
an arm and leg both numb,
paralysis for emotion.

Who's welcome to him now?
Misfortune volunteered
to place a stepmother into
my stricken father's family.
They made a moving twosome.
But to this day I long

for a booth in the ice cream shop
with posters on the wall
of colored scoops, waffle cones,
and with my younger brother
enjoy the man alone.
I want it all.

Summer Rental

Stately on its promontory,
it sits in distant memory
like columned colonnades in myths
from barely educated youth.
Make of it what we will:
the seascapes on the walls
tell of what might have been,
had we been more securely born,
or made our living from the sea
aloof to down east luxury.
We covet on the wooden wall
the sleek Concordia yawl
moored in its obliging cove
and hallowed in its honored alcove.
Nostalgia everywhere abounds
in upstairs rooms, or bound
in albums, torn and stored,
intended found rewards
among the many tattered books
on shelves, among the nooks
and crannies of a week away.
And charts, the charts!—of bay
and reach; our spot, like wrecks,
marked with a scarlet X.
Our spot, indeed. We rent
a touch of wanted seaside scent
to complement the crash of wave
on stone. And yes, it's ours to have,
the fragrance, feel and tone
enough for now, if not our own.

On the Yacht Namouna

after Julius LeBlanc Stewart's painting, Venice,
1890, Wadsworth Atheneum, Hartford, CT

Only the sailor sees the open sea,
the others, five in number, more involved
with something none of us will ever see
or know. How have these several lives evolved
    to settle here and let the ocean air
      drive from their faces any clue of care?

Should we suppose the painter to be part
of a three-couple excursion, engaged,
perhaps, to one young woman on this yacht,
within a picture he himself has staged?
    If so, the women on the left are meant,
      the woman on the right much too content

within her thoughts, a dog's head in her lap,
her husband too engrossed within his book—
or thus assumptions might easily unwrap
a scene like this, following one long look.
    Is not the interest on the other side?
      Look here to find a sweetheart or a bride.

Things, relatively speaking, are unsteady—
two women and a man—all three—must find
support from something solid, at the ready—
a chair, an arm, a rail all grasped behind
    as one might stage a woman at her ease,
      a man uneasily; and if you please,

what has the woman in the chair just said?
And don't we wish to *see* the face (kept turned
away) the man enjoys? (Her hair's the red
of the mahogany behind her.) Unconcerned,
   the sailor is alone in knowing how
   the best of views is off the starboard bow.

Heart

Who would, on having seen a pumping heart,
a knotted fist of stubborn shiny gristle—
yes, *who* could possibly compare it to
the feeling on a close to perfect day
of walking hand in hand madly in love?

Is pumping blood the proper sign of love—
blood in, blood out—and who has never thought
about the places all that blood has been?
"Please! Have a heart," the saying goes.
Why not a liver, or a brain, a bowel?

And why make such a silly symbol stand
for love—a question mark without its dot
admiring so its own reflection? No.
I think I'll save my heart for pumping blood,
in case by clotting it with too much love
I break a necessary thing in two.

Stone Cottage

A childhood vision of a life
spent in a grey stone cottage north
of anywhere he'd lived before,
entails expansive views of sea,
and in the currency of memory
worth more than those he'd stored away
dozing in southern latitudes.
Star-bright winters, arctic cold,
tease nerveless reaches of his mind
to give him what he'd never had:
a sharp, hardscrabble life without
the need to be there, or to suffer.

Winter Room

The fire burns as the fire has burned before,
but the antique clock stands mutely by the door.
The portraits of the children stare at me
before our hallowed mountains, and the sea.
"Be happy," say the children in their frames.
The winter drafts play wintry sorts of games.
A whispered imitation of a roar,
the fire still burns as fire has burned before.
The portraits on the wall are mute; as are
the familiar, odd attempts of family art.
There they'll stay beyond the day I leave,
if only as the memories I conceive.
The fire burns as fire has burned before.

Nap

The moment when I fall asleep,
a fleeting second's mystery
of nothing's pale trajectory—

it will come…will come…and yet
in retrospect, it is as lost to time
as any second we forget.

And then the inner waking, eyes
still closed…the presence of a working brain…
and now to know…to realize…
all the commitments for the day remain.

Snow Patches in Rain

Stragglers of a late snowfall
cast their last
fog that, all but swept away by mist
in exhalations of despair,
dismisses in the winter air
what next year's winter will recall.

II. Mind's Eye

Mind's Eye

What is it that we see with the eyes closed?
A drawing by a child? A Rorschach blot;
a bust of some forgotten relative
as dead as Roman statuary?
None of these—but a ghost at best, restive
to get on with things, rejoin the gallery
of faces you adore, yet can hardly see.
Take the face that you have known the best:
now place it on the desk by her portrait;
let it hover there, a likeness of a likeness:
reality must swallow whole the human ghost.

Pilot Light

A twist of the wrist is all it takes
to start the day, transfer the spark,
the morning dark,
to a ring of fire. The stove awakes

into a useful burn
one burner at a time. The boil,
the bake, the broil—
each takes its turn

to propagate incendiary flame,
and all from this one light,
its only expertise: ignite.
Words are much the same.

Highboy

That day, I held somewhere within my head
the structure of a highboy, memorized in bed,
joint by joint by joint. How the apron notched
into the leg, how drawers had to be matched
in pleasant graduations, and the frames
supporting them—the pieces and their names—
all, I tediously learned until the whole
damn thing made sense from cove to cabriole.

But when divorced from diagram and page
of what—in thinking in this abstract stage—
did images of mind in fact consist?
Were they lines and curves of a synthesist
inflection now transmuted to a form—
the true *Ursache* of the diagram?

Or was it some imperfect sense of mind
that lines to vague particulars consigned?
Some twenty years have passed since printed plans
transferred to me this complex elegance;
they are clear still. Yet I would not dare pretend
that what mind sees I'll ever comprehend.

Going, Going, Gone

Our exiled denizen from a better day,
from a grander room, a nobler city home,
a chest on stand (a *highboy* she would say)
in eighteenth century mahogany, from some

chandeliered, long-tabled dining room
where sisters—four, then three—once used to play
(I can, from other things I know, assume)
till death and marriage sent them all away.

The Great Depression, if I heard her right,
made challenges for them all…the legacy
of Brookline splendor turned to a sorry sight
of comic, boxed-in aristocracy.

A Philadelphia highboy, she once bragged,
knowing I knew nothing and didn't care,
though later on, in an antiques magazine
its twin appeared, a svelte Queen Anne affair

with provenance to match. And then the shame
from having sold what better eyes demand
to save, not sell; and then the dull self-blame
for having grandeur taken off my hands.

Here, my once proud mother, bent with age,
sits in the only photo left to me,
where graceful proof of Brookline heritage
sits behind her every day with dignity.

Antiques

The market—according to a friend—has tanked
for—as he termed it—all "brown furniture."
The young, apparently, have had enough
of all this glaring-down of gloom, the
dark mahogany, walnut, shellacked
to deep, suggestive moods of swirling grain.
Perhaps it's just the shift of generations.
Mine loved carved fans and finials, their cases
standing sturdily against the wall.
Those brasses, too, dulled by our negligence,
used to sparkle in the candlelight.
Three-hundred-year-old work deserves to shine.

Boot Jack

The oldest thing I own,
two rough-hewn scraps of wood:
one cut to grip the boot
snug to the ankle bone,

then nailed to an angled block
with hand-forged nails (and three
banged in more recently
from cut-nail hardware stock).

Some country craftsman's eye
saw in the needed use
a whimsical excuse
to hone and dignify:

for such a crude device
it has a fine detail,
makes of a swallow's tail
a grip of strength and grace.

But for its grace, I doubt
this jack would now exist,
endure a move, resist
the urge to throw it out.

Three hundred years and more
it's come through to fulfill
a task it's up to still,
stationed by the door.

From Where This Silence Settled

The silence was respectful, so
I let it settle on me like a cat,
his eyes closed, sleeping where I sat.
Any purr would be too loud.

From *where* this silence settled I can't tell;
perhaps it was the noise I'd scared away.
Silence has its own queer kind of spell.

More Word than Meaning

The immaterial essence when I die,
as if the smoke had not derived from fire,
the fire from some spontaneous desire,
urges me to prolong life with lies.

But *soul* would make me more than what I am,
more than poet, father, spouse, composer—
all of which together come much closer
than any verbal ghost or hologram

that ties me up into a wraithful role;
although I must admit that every time
I struggle for a noun to make all mine,
for "man" or "one," I much prefer a "soul."

Train Travel

Something about a town seen from the train—
the station plaque, the hiss of halting steam—
that sets imagination into dream.
Distorted in the glint of streaming rain,

a man, seen through the window, stores his bike
just out of view. No person disembarks.
As we inch forward ready to depart
a view across the hills and meadows strikes

familiar notes of longing, undefined,
for idylls where a lifelong search might end.
Dreams of vague fulfillment around a bend
of track are quickly passed and left behind.

The vision, not the place, must now persist,
the final station on the line in view,
as occupations of the day renew,
restore, ingrain what scenery resists.

Returning to the route that brought us here,
consulting maps for answers, even clues
prove futile. All we have are teasing views;
all there is of place is atmosphere.

Dreamless Sleep

This little patch of death without a dream
transported me from darkened rooms last night
to dump me back within the window's gleam,
to ponder last night's vacuum in hindsight.

But how to ponder nothing afterward,
or anytime at all, is but to talk
of blank stillness beyond a sounding chord,
or boulevards where ghosts are said to walk.

We cannot even call this blank a taste
of death, a handout from eternity,
but just a swath of consciousness erased
within a life where something used to be.

Death is a gift of nothing, then, a void
we dream and never know to wake and know;
death is, at life's end, one last thought destroyed
from which from nothing nothingness will grow.

III. Unearthing My Fossil

Life: Darwin Explained

In the beginning, just
one pip of matter, stocked
with carbon, zest—robust,
inevitably locked.

A billion years go by;
one speck, at last, alive,
then two, then more, which try
just to survive.

The Grand Cannibal

Like swarms of hornets to a paper ball,
the earth's hungriest species grasp and cling,
masticate, devour, fly and crawl,
inflict with deadly poison, bite and sting,
in order that the living remain able
to keep supplies of protein on the table.

Hunger and the Hawk

Hunger knows the hawk and what it wants;
the hawk knows hunger: it is himself.

Credo in Short Sentences

I exist. My back
I cannot see is there.
Eternity,
and even air,
hidden from me,
exist. The lack

of proof is not a proof.
From matter comes
the flesh, from flesh
ideas. Large sums
of matter mesh
in tight, aloof.

But all along
things change. I change.
Ideas foster doubt.
The All, its range,
could toss the whole thing out.
I could be wrong.

Notes from Underground

How much it takes to make a go of things:
a quick scratch in your burrow, and a rock—
no hint of it till now—forces a retreat.
Detour defines the logbook of a life.

To work the topsoil tunnels like a vole,
the love of underground so freely yours
to sniff around in, day or night! So where
would pleasure stop? There's that rock again.

Unearthing My Fossil

… how I got to be so far away
is not for *me* to know; I died
at least a lonely thousand years ago,
where wind and water took their time, but that
was 2053. The oldest graves
are gone. The river dried up long ago—
but this is all conjecture—see how earth
forgets its kin…why they found fingers first
is not for *me* to say: these guys, I guess,
know best. *These* finger bones are here to stay.
It took *at least* a thousand years; don't think
I don't appreciate the manicure,
the way you clear the sand away—who knows
what sediments took over, clearing flesh
from bone—the way you fuss and fuss at knuckles,
one at a time. I can't recall just how
it felt to have the ancient desert streams—
so *rare* the desert streams—clear flesh from bone.
Another eon beckons me away.

~

How peaceful it has been, away from fear.
The sun cools down to nothing in the night.
Although to you this romance in the sun
is one long dropping-out of time; note, please,
the evidence longevity gives a skull,
my skull. What makes you want me so?
Leave the spine alone, a silent plea
I made in life as well. I thought in life:
There'll be a day, when to lie back in the sun
will be the very last vestigial wish
a man might, as his rightful due, expect.
Who'd ever think of *this?* The evening breeze

makes overtures to lure me back to life,
but early though it is, it is too late.

~

The faith you have in learning from the dead!
Look me in the cavities that were my eyes,
but you won't find the sediments that washed
away, and washed away again …
How slow the human race is to move on!

~

You all keep reading so much into me—
easy does it! If only I could answer
the questions you keep asking one another.
What human rights have I a hope of—what's
the word?—"enjoying" hardly fits—when fingers
are packed away to leave the rest of me
to elementary eternity?

Why not take all of me?—why are you laughing?
Even here in the desert there were rumors;
how even the most careful burial
can never quite assure eternal rest—
and tell me, all you scientists in shorts,
where will you take me when you're through with this?

The vehicles have arrived, I see—if that
is what they are. How carefully you lift me,
my ribs and skull, I could be just a baby—
Easy does it! Is this an ambulance?
We had those once—so when did all those wheels
give up their function to the cushioned air?

The next phase now begins. Will other bones
now lure you all away? Will my top half
be laid out on display with all the rest?

~

Yes, set me down—I'm dizzy from the drive—
Not here! Bones are everywhere—one never knows
with whom I'll be expected to get along—
yes, here—if you could dim the light a little,
but not too dim; some clarity is welcome
after so many years.
From shifting sands back to cold burnished steel.
After all these years they still use drawers!
One always has nostalgia for the sand—
if friends could hear me now!
Or see me photogenically exposed.
If I were flesh, there'd surely be a law
against this ghoulishness.
      "It's time for lunch,"
an old man says, pointing at his watch,
reviving hunger for an appetite
I haven't thought about in years. Light's out,
and away they go. Abandonment again …

~

People are so noisy after lunch—
have I slept that long?—Is that a whiff
of alcohol?—"It's time," one fellow says.
"Like packing eggs," another says; they laugh.
Now in the drawer. The steel, as I've just said,

is cold, so cold. Will any of them think
to say farewell? The shrinking rectangle
of fluorescent light diminishes to black;
I hear the lab door close; the silence gathers
around me once again, and so:
                                      Good night.

A Sailing Out from Life

The surges of a joy
are all that joy entails:
a sailing out from life
with reefed and rounded sails
from someplace never safe,
whether home or Troy.

Remember to come home
to where shared action is,
where interests still accrue,
the games of hers and his—
but leave a year or two
to build another Rome.

IV. Flight

Hummingbird

A jeweled artifact,
making the most of air,
of movement, hovers where
its quick flights attract

my eye to columbine.
It lingers or it darts
in delicate false starts,
its flight a stitched design.

But having had its fill,
this gem of priceless things
steals off in a blur of wings,
a moment's summer thrill.

Blackbird on a Cattail

Look, how the captain of his perch
faces weather, blown about.
What does a bird think of the shout
of wind, of chaos all around?

And then, as this one did, fly off
buoyed by a faith, his course
determined by a heavy gust,
an updraft or a microburst,
the forces any flyer must
calculate to keep aloft.

Fish

Who knows what thoughts you entertain,
your only form of utterance
an open mouth and a blank stare?
What we take for dull-witted trance
may be the damming up of pain.

Their World

Birds take for granted air,
fish water. Nothing's there

is what they probably think,
until fish take a drink;

but even then I doubt
they stop to ask about

what's clearly everywhere:
water clear as air,

or air, a nothing and
so hard to understand

no bird will even try.
It's hard enough to fly.

Invisibility
is very hard to see.

Testing North in February

As if elusions from a fairy tale,
the evidence of birds—a note or two
from a woodland up the road—a flash of red
on a blackbird's wing—the first few hints of hope:
scouts sent forth from an optimistic south.

Or are they just this year's equivalent
of avian explorers of the poles?
Conductors of reconnaissance for cats
bivouacked with a flock of respective kin,
alert to future wood and worm and seed
before the full invasion settles in?

Above the Arctic Ice

*If you could say it in words there would
be no reason to paint.*
—Edward Hopper

Had curlicues of pencil half the wit
of dreams that infiltrate the early hours
they'd dictate *all* my dreams:
in sleep, my brain has forty times the power.

To capture such elusive fantasy!
As futile as transliterating Bach—
replacing perfect counterpoint with words.
Or trying to improve what music lacks.
We might as well replace the wings of birds
with fins or webs or frantic gadgetry.

No. Trust the pencil point to twists and turns,
to make the search of meaning effortless
free flight, untethered as the Arctic tern.

Baltimore Visitors, 2021

The pair of orioles that searched our apple tree
for food, the yard for twigs and twine to build a nest,
have flown away. Our tree, our yard, have failed the test,
as they did last year. Now, again, we'll miss their sweetly

tempered voices filtering down from taller trees.
They have us slow our step, and make the mundane walk
to get the mail a thrill. For them it's just small talk,
for us, to be arrested by a moment's will to please.

V. Settling on the View

Meeting on the Stairs

"The view from ninety is magnificent."
He was four steps above me when he said it,
I on my way up, he coming down.
His smile was radiant, a testament
delivered in a two-man traffic jam.
His age I couldn't quite imagine then,
or if I could—my memory of him is vague,
thanks to my now being eighty—has left
for parts unknown. His smile was full of teeth,
the kindest teeth I'd ever seen. A friend—
I'd made a friend without a word exchanged.
I stared a moment, not because of who
among the family of guests he was—
I had not read him then, nor heard the myths.
We stood a moment on the narrow stairs
before I must have backed the few steps down
to let him slowly pass. He disappeared
soon after that. "A neighbor," I was told.

Divestiture

The day will come—it's not that far ahead—
when tripping on the stairs, or on the walk,
the simple function of the knee, the toe,
or just an early morning need to pee
will bring the whole thing down.

The stairs that seemed so quaint in middle age
now scream for railings. Snow has gained in weight,
or so it seems. The chairs around the house,
the ones I still enjoy, invite me in
for longer stays than health, in fact, approves.
The comforts of our home invite a move.

Many friends and relatives I know
enjoy now sparer lives. Their libraries,
reduced by half, and half again and more,
have shrunk, accommodating aging eyes.

Dwindled, too, the senses that import
the world's ambiguous detail:
the thin, repeated dactyls of the sparrow
heard as digital replies, if heard at all.

Proper Nouns Are the First to Go

The names of people fly off randomly,
tag-sale labels blown away by wind,
un-retrieved, or, with work and luck, found
in the nick of time and greeted with a smile.
Only later do we realize
that ours had made an early exit too.
We gather up as quickly as we can
just what it was we had in mind to say.

Your face is so familiar; who you are
I've known for more than thirty, forty years.
Yet that by which you are well known—by the bank,
the DMV, your wife—is lost to me:
when it comes to greeting you I draw a blank.
Oh, for a fairer system, whereby we
can call each other any name we want,
a name reflective of the mood and moment.

I tire of my excuses: how my sleep
buries another name each night, or how
someone nightly steals my frontal lobes.
I mix you up, though never *who* you are.
To use the tag-sale loss that started this,
the china remains the china, the glass the glass.
Better, that we smile at our defeat,
forget the names, and let the moment pass.

Eighty's the New Sixty

I was, of course, inclined to jump for joy,
to hear, at my age, of the gradual loss
of subcutaneous fat—was it a ploy
to rid me of the guilt from eating sauce,
or other things that like to hibernate
between my liver-spotted skin and bone?
Alas, along with gradual loss of weight
came symptoms I'm less eager to condone,
as when I need the furnace to deliver
a blast of warmer air before its time,
to stop my bony body's need to shiver.
And this when temperatures are said to climb!
80 is now 60, I heard this noon;
let winter be like summer, then, and soon.

Spring Day, 2020

What is a spring day
without something to worry about—
a family debt,
a neighbor on her way.

And now this,
a modern plague
to make of every ache a vague
symptom of the virus.

Let's hope for another false alarm.
We wash our raw and reddened hands
as often as the protocol demands.
We stay calm.

Forsythia invades the town,
thanks to spring sun. Again,
wind, and with it, a hint of rain.
We hunker down.

March Ahead

The coy and hesitating spring begins
as sky that any optimist could wish for,
while we survive and *thrive* in quarantine.
But don't despair; the force that slowly fills
a blade of grass with green—an infectious green
allowing fields all they once have been—
will march ahead to claim the distant hills.

Obituary Picture, 2021

Appointments missed can circle back to haunt you.
Let one I broke so many years ago
serve as example—we were soon to part—
you to some distant place—to college? No,
to an apprenticeship? A wooded park
in North Dakota, say, or Timbuktu?

You had that wayward look of worried sons
when the future refuses comforts of the home
—the less-than-satisfactory familiar—
when urgencies of some dark chromosome,
entwined around the quickened thoughts of failure,
beckon boys to limitless horizons.

Another look said all I had to know—
of promises I made to sit with you,
to talk about how the future might allow
for dreams I might have helped you to pursue—
for fertile seeds I might have helped you sow.

That would have been some twenty years ago.

Is Every Death Our Own?

Is every death our own,
with all we have to lose,
with all we have to say?
The world is mainly loss,
our voices die away,
now heard, now soft, now gone.

Alone

I was not there for you,
alone in your corner,
the sentence passed without me.
Leaving, did you still see
one last solemn mourner
as a last remembered view?

No matter what we say,
the milk, the toys, the tears,
the love affairs, the beddings,
the unsuccessful weddings,
successful lost careers,
lead up to this one day.

We offer up clichés:
you can't go home again;
this will be your last bed
(without it being said).
Thoughts linger there, and then:
let me count the ways

I've failed you once again:
you died alone that night
and something in me, too,
dies to think of you,
alone, so small with fright,
an hour, maybe two, then gone.

Settling

He might as well have built a wall around himself,
refusing, as he does, to use his hearing aid.
His ancient model, a leech-like thing, lies on the shelf
above his head. "Here, plug the damn thing in," I've said

as often as he's mumbled something back to me.
I ask him what he said, before he's gone again,
but something like a childish pout is his reply:
"At my age understanding's hardly worth the pain!"

All he said, of course, was how it hurt his ear,
the old complaints I'd be unlikely to pursue.
He said it loud enough for buried folk to hear,
so I sat quietly and settled on the view.

Sculpture Garden

A settled elder, poverty on view,
the barn out back sits nestled in among
the castoffs of a generation too
busy with its lives of grain and dung

to tidy up the remnants left behind.
The old greenhouse, reduced to hoops and slab,
has stood for years, abandonment defined.
Two farm trucks and a stack of boards stand by.

A garden view, I heard a neighbor call it;
his voice—it had a kind of vacant sound.
The barn looks on, as it's inclined to do,
awaits the season's hay, and holds its ground.

Refrain

You seek solace from the pain's command,
a voice of sympathy so sweet and pure
it sings and swallows grief without the cure
of time and distance pain demands.

A melody of such compelling grace,
it winds its way to sources of your grief,
once there, refuses you sought-for relief—
and yet, you'd trade this for no other place.

Give thanks. Imbibe its dark liqueur,
and welcome its infusion for your grief,
leaving you, if still awaiting time's relief,
a little less despondent where you were.

Wake

Sound travels with hushed importance
across the bay from Scott Island,
a calm drone of inboard burble
anticipating the higher pitch of power.
The wake slaps at this patch of shore,
a reminder of routine passage.
The bay, a grey reflection of the sky
flattened to a palimpsest of ripple,
rock and sail, covers its tracks,
leaving to my imagination the tracery
of all my father's father's summer routes.
His craft still passes Two Bush Island,
Hog Island's northeast spruce astern,
retired like its pilot ancestor
to the black and white of the photograph
hanging on my father's bedroom wall.
A trackless passage defines us all.

VI. Column Two

A Fortune Turned

Make no mistake about it, when
there's money to be made, a hand
will find its way now and again
   to beg for or demand.

The one from need, the other from
the knowledge less will flow to more;
the one in need of any crumb,
   the other rich and bored.

A penny saved's a penny earned,
they feel the same in any fist;
to save is but a fortune turned
   from where it will be missed.

Not Far from Here

Not far from here a farmer likes to hunt.
He cleans and skins the carcasses himself
(but not until he hangs them out to dry,
to season them I think's the reason why).

If only he could add a hint of grace
to his front-yard-deer-carcass-hanging place;
please, neighbors, won't you all impress on him
not to use his children's jungle gym.

Broken Glass

What could be sadder than a place
where death rolled through, a ton
of hurtling steel into the sun,
where racing blindness met disgrace

and two young children playing there
are now replaced by nothing we
can recognize with certainty
but broken glass and blank despair?

Scandal

First the hint that something's wrong:
the woman's name in column two—
no charges filed, although a few
bold claims suspected all along …

How skillfully she played her parts
and now this charge—to mix the shame
of cash and bribe with her good name,
her housewives, goddesses and tarts.

Now, no one dares to sing her praise,
yet to forgive (and soon), as you,
once guilty, begged them do for you,
stirs new regrets among malaise.

Background Music

What was it that determined no event,
no item advertised on any screen,
no opportunity of peace where we
prefer an intimate and quiet meal,
no picture of a venture into space
past Saturn or past Mars, black holes,
past galaxy on galaxy of dust,
detritus, gases, rocks, hell-sent debris
the universe coughs up for our delight—

no cinematic meetings of the lips,
or shots of distant mountains in the sun,
the ocean's power, the insect's nervous twitch—

Who decreed we drench this all in music,
in sounds that make each of us out front
just one of Pavlov's salivating dogs,
with distant growls, with fearful pedal tones
to "reinforce" grim documentaries,
with landfill after landfill of cliché—

all I ask, if only for a day,
is for the myriad purveyors of the noise
behind the noise, on call, online, on hold,
to please consider—if just for this one day—
turning every note of background off!

Compose a Fugue: A Practical Guide

Nothing is more practical today—
or any day of this or any year—
than, when your mind is innocently clear,
to contemplate, compose and then to play

a composition lithe and strict of style.
Invent a subject no one will forget,
and follow with an answer, securely set;
employ the pair, include each voice, beguile

us with your contrapuntal skill, and weave
among the expositions episodes
related by their motifs and their modes;
add a thematic cadence, then take your leave.

Nothing humans do can take the place
of satisfaction born of mental grace.

Noon to Midnight

A masterwork lay shining up ahead,
the sun still at its highest in the sky;
the best of me, still ruefully unsaid,
had all the afternoon to fructify.

The afternoon proved friendly to the plan,
if falling somewhat short of expectations.
My projects suited a much more gifted man,
and midnight loomed to dampen aspirations.

Now, evening slides on by me with the ease
that age and weariness resign me to,
reminding me my powers are all too few,
constricting, still, what one full day achieves.

Just the Bay

The bay before me now is just the bay;
the wind is up, the sails are taut with it;
the bathers, having had enough of sun,
tote baggage up the path near where I sit.
A ferry in the distance works its way
from city wharves, hidden behind the trees,
to a landing by a village on a hill.
A horn announcing fog I long to see
repeats its sorry monotone, yet still,
how many playful ghosts of summer fun
invade this sultry afternoon. But I
no longer want to sail—were I to try,
the smallest wave would heave me in the drink!
Much easier now to look, to dream and think.

About the Author

Composer Donald Wheelock, Irwin and Pauline Alper Glass Professor Emeritus of Music at Smith College, began writing poems in his twenties, often for the purpose of setting them to music. Many of his poems soon declared their independence from that purpose, however. In the last few years, he has revived some of those early poems to add to the many he has recently written, successfully submitting them to publications that welcome formal poetry. His chapbook, *In the Sea of Dreams,* is available through Gallery of Readers Press. *It's Hard Enough to Fly* is his first full-length book of poems. His musical works include chamber, vocal and orchestral music. He has received awards, as a composer, from the National Endowment for the Arts and the Guggenheim Foundation. He lives with his wife Anne in Whately, Massachusetts.

www.ingramcontent.com/pod-product-compliance
Lightning Source LLC
Chambersburg PA
CBHW070937160426
43193CB00011B/1714